MUDRAS

Healing with Vibrant Hands

Cairo P Rocha, OMD, PhD

Balboa Press books may be ordered through booksellers or by contacting:

Balboa Press
A Division of Hay House
1663 Liberty Drive
Bloomington, IN 47403
www.balboapress.com
1 (877) 407-4847

Because of the dynamic nature of the Internet, any web addresses or links contained in
this book may have changed since publication and may no longer be valid. The views
expressed in this work are solely those of the author and do not necessarily reflect the views
of the publisher, and the publisher hereby disclaims any responsibility for them.

Any people depicted in stock imagery provided by Getty Images are models,
and such images are being used for illustrative purposes only.
Certain stock imagery © Getty Images.

ISBN: 978-1-5043-9958-6 (sc)
ISBN: 978-1-5043-9959-3 (e)

Library of Congress Control Number: 2018903273

Print information available on the last page.

Balboa Press rev. date: 06/19/2018

Preface

Mudras came into my life in an interesting and unexpected way. Many years ago, while doing my four-year acupuncture training in Japan, it came to my knowledge that occasionally courses on Tibetan Medicine were offered to foreign health care practitioners in Dharamsala, Northern India. For many years, I tried contacting the Tibetan Institute about the possibility of attending one of their courses but wasn't successful. However, in 2007, I got a message saying that a course was scheduled to take place in the following year and that I was welcome to attend it.

The following spring, I went to Men-Tsee-Khang, the Tibetan Medical and Astrological Institute in Dharamsala with a group of foreign students where we were exposed to the foundations and highlights of Tibetan Medicine. Prior to that experience, I had regarded Chinese medicine as the broadest and most encompassing system of medicine as it includes the body, mind and emotions. I was soon to find out, to my delight, that Tibetan Medicine goes one notch further or higher: the concept of Compassion! As a result, at every stage of a herbal formula preparation, there is always a mantra or prayer being sung so as to infuse the remedy with compassion and high vibrations.

The school where the course was taking place was decorated

with a variety of statues of Tibetan-Buddhist deities and I noticed that each one was portrayed with different gestures and hand positions. (Fig. 1 and 2 – Buddha). For some reason, this interesting observation stayed with me throughout the days I spent at the school.

After the course, I went to Laddak, also called Indian Tibet, where I stayed for over one week visiting a variety of ancient monasteries. The flight to Leh, the capital of Laddak, was quite a unique experience because, after about two hours flying over the endless snowy Himalayans, the plane takes a turn and descends on a clearing. We landed!

On the very first night, while I was in my hotel room preparing to go to sleep, I opened a zipper of a compartment in my suitcase looking for a plastic bag and, to my surprise out came a book on Mudras! I was taken aback because I had no recollection of having bought that book and much less what it was doing in my suitcase all the way to the Himalayans! Amazed, I browsed through the pages that showed different hand gestures and postures. Then, feeling tired, I went to sleep and what happened next was close to surreal: I woke up in the middle of the night wide-eyed and bushy tailed and sat in the bed. It felt as if something had short circuited my brain. All of a sudden everything started to make sense to me: the hand gestures or mudras depicted by the deities were more than just artistic creations, they convey a message. By using my knowledge of Chinese medicine I realized that, more than anything else, the Mudras were therapeutic tools! I, then, took a notebook and wrote very quickly a few pages with thoughts and insights that were coming to me. Thus, I might say that the material you are reading was "downloaded" at that moment

Mudras

Besides the facial muscles, no other part of the human anatomy expresses emotions as perfectly as the hands. Our hands are capable of conveying our thoughts and feelings in a precise and detailed way through a wide range of gestures and movements. Tight fists signify tension and anger, shaking hands mean fear, and perspiring or 'nervous' hands reveal worry, for example. The Chinese believe that the hands are an extension of the Heart, and since the Heart is considered to be the seat of the Mind, it is understandable that gentle and harmonious gestures reflect a peaceful Mind. On the other hand, a disturbed Heart (Mind) is the underlying cause behind aggressive, agitated and uncontrolled hand movements.

Throughout our lives we rely on our hands to perform a myriad functions ranging from basic skills like feeding ourselves to the most subtle and elevated expressions of our being, like healing and praying. The many nerve endings covering the surfaces of the hands are responsible for one of our most basic and refined senses — the tactile sense. In fact, the area associated with the hands in our cerebral cortex is large, which confirms the sensory importance given to the hands and fingers. (Fig.3 – Cerebral Cortex) Through evolution, the human brain has developed a profusion of neurological connections that control the hands and finger movements. One of the most fascinating traditions of using the hands for therapeutic purposes — Mudras — comes from India. For thousands of years, yogis have used these specific hand and finger postures with the purpose of stimulating the brain, healing the body-mind and expanding consciousness

Interestingly, modern scientists have recently demonstrated that repeatedly moving and exercising the fingers in the Mudra fashion stimulates a large portion of the brain. It causes a significant increase in neuron renewal as well as expansion of the neuronal network, especially in the motor cortex of the brain, which controls movement and general physical coordination. The Mudras enhance the energy flow in the body through the meridians, or *nadis* (energy channels), the terminal points of which are located in the fingers, as well as in the feet. Mudras help to create inner peace and strength, eliminate tiredness, anxiety, and improve physical and emotional health. Ideally, the Mudras should be practiced seated, with the legs crossed in the traditional meditative posture. However, they are effective even if a person performs them while walking with the hands in the pockets, or lying down.

Some sources suggest that Mudras should be practiced for 30 minutes daily, while others recommend 15 minutes three times a day, or until the health issue being addressed subsides.

In summary, the Mudras help to:

- Bring about peace and harmony

- Increase the body's power to heal

- Considerably improve cognitive function

- Promote change in an individual's fundamental outlook, both in regard to his/her health and to life in general

- Elevate a person in all aspects: physical, mental, emotional and spiritual.

ANJALI

**The palms of both hands are united
at the center of the chest.**

- salutation

- the brain's left and right hemispheres meet at
the heart level

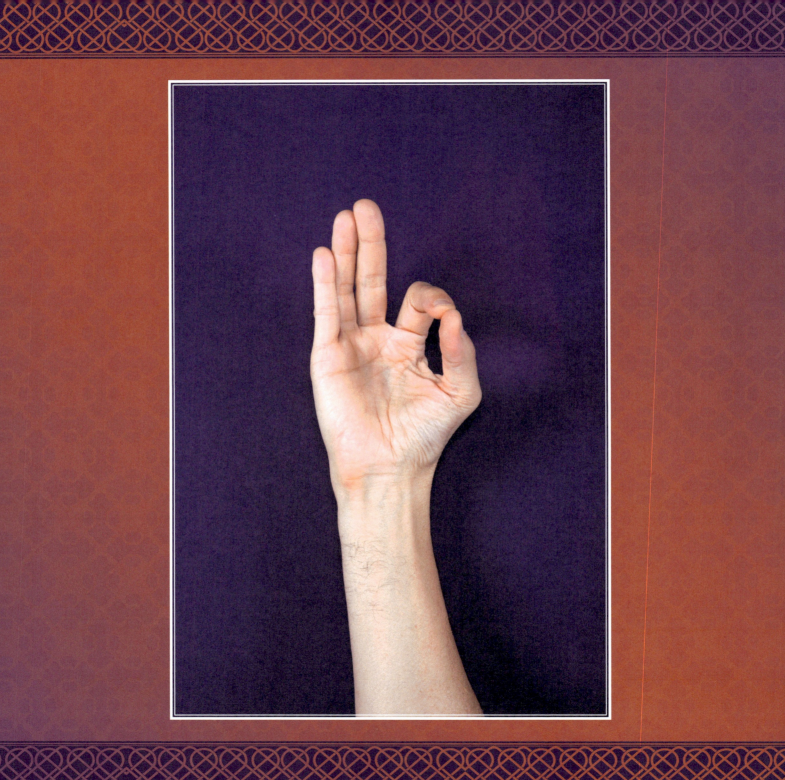

JNANA

**The tips of the thumb and index finger gently touch.
The other fingers are together and pointing upwards.**

- sends energy to the brain

- improves memory

- releases mental stress

- alleviates insomnia

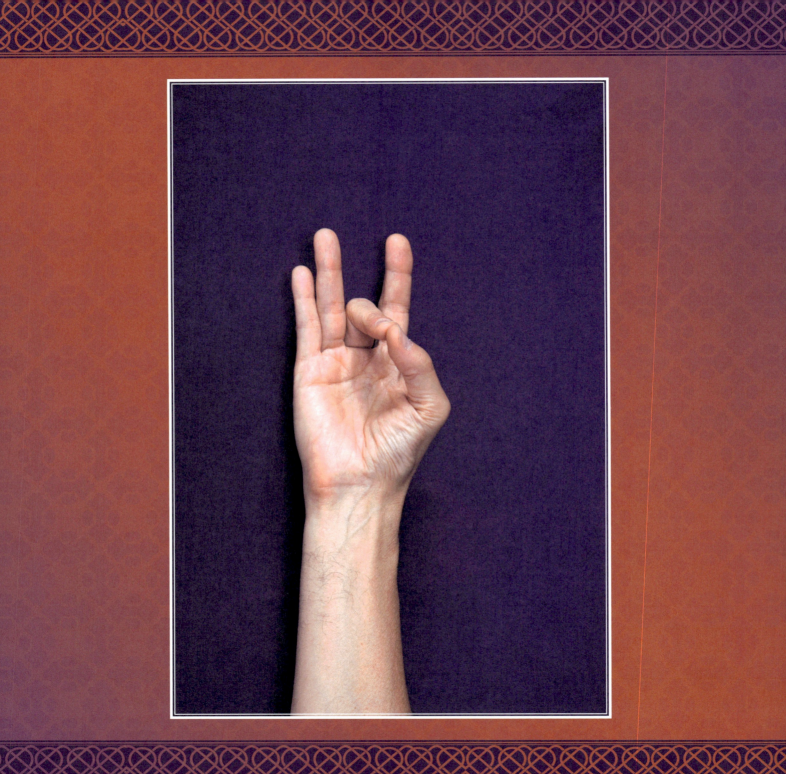

AKASHA

**The tips of the thumb and middle finger gently touch.
The other fingers are straight and pointing upwards.**

- helps with heart conditions

- strengthens the bones

- improves the production of blood

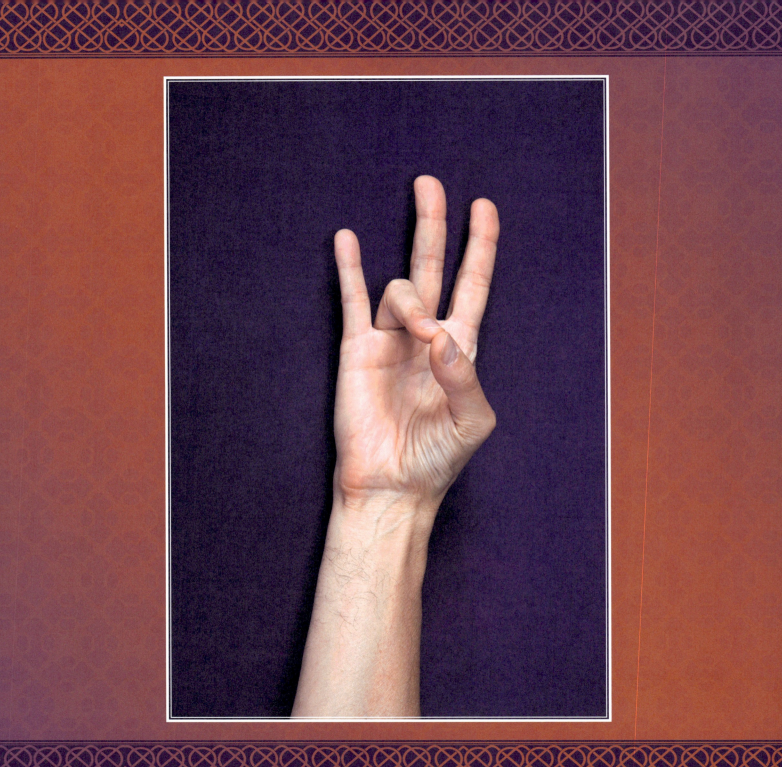

PRITWI

The tips of the thumb and the ring finger gently touch. The other fingers are straight and pointing upwards.

- increases energy

- promotes weight loss

- improves the skin

- induces peace of mind

VARUNA (BUDHI)

The tips of the thumb and the little finger gently touch. The other fingers are together and pointing upwards.

- promotes body hydration

- cools the body

- stimulates blood purification

- heals gastric ailments

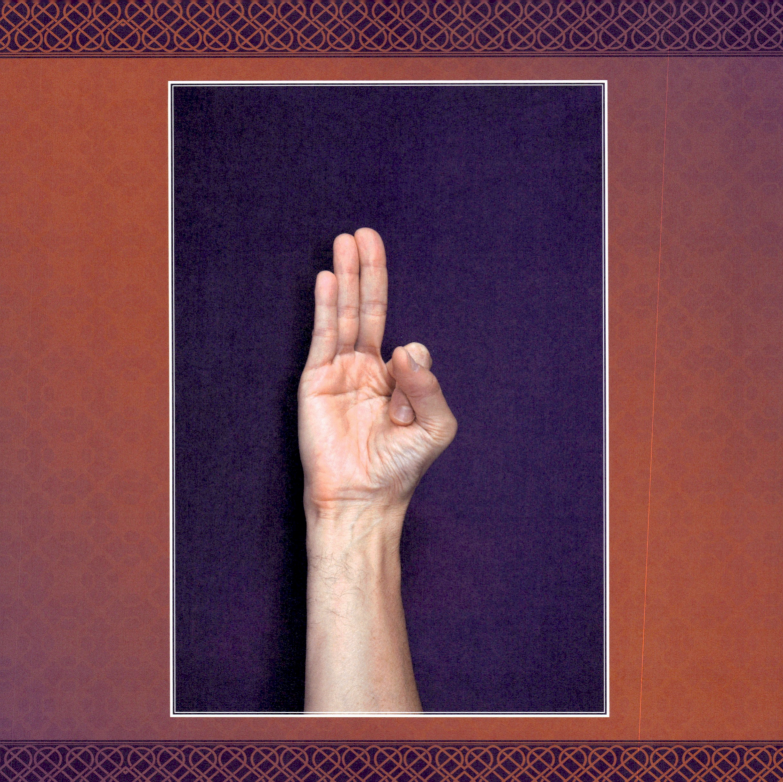

VAYU

The index finger is bent, touching the base of the thumb, and the thumb is gently placed over it. The other fingers are together and pointing upwards.

- heals joint pain, arthritis, rheumatism and stiff neck

- helps with facial paralysis

- treats flatulence

SHUNYA

The middle finger is bent, touching the base of the thumb, and the thumb is gently placed over it. The other fingers are straight and pointing upwards.

- assists with ear problems

- treats deafness

SURYA

The ring finger is bent, touching the base of the thumb, and the thumb is gently placed over it. The other fingers are straight and pointing upwards.

- activates the thyroid gland

- treats lung-related problems (asthma, etc.)

- improves digestion

- eases tension

- promotes weight loss

JALODAMASHAKA

The little finger is bent, touching the base of the thumb, and the thumb is gently placed over it. The other fingers are together and pointing upwards.

- treats urinary problems, water retention and dehydration

- helps heal a sore throat

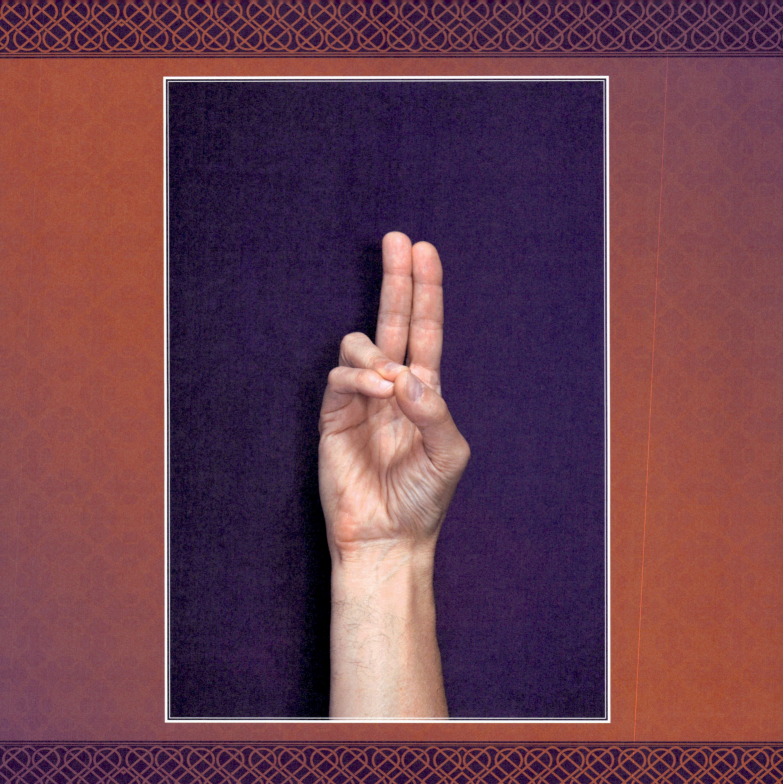

PRANA

The tips of the little and ring fingers gently touch the tip of the thumb. The other fingers are straight and pointing upwards.

- improves sight

- promotes blood circulation

- increases vitality

- strengthens the immune system

- activates energy

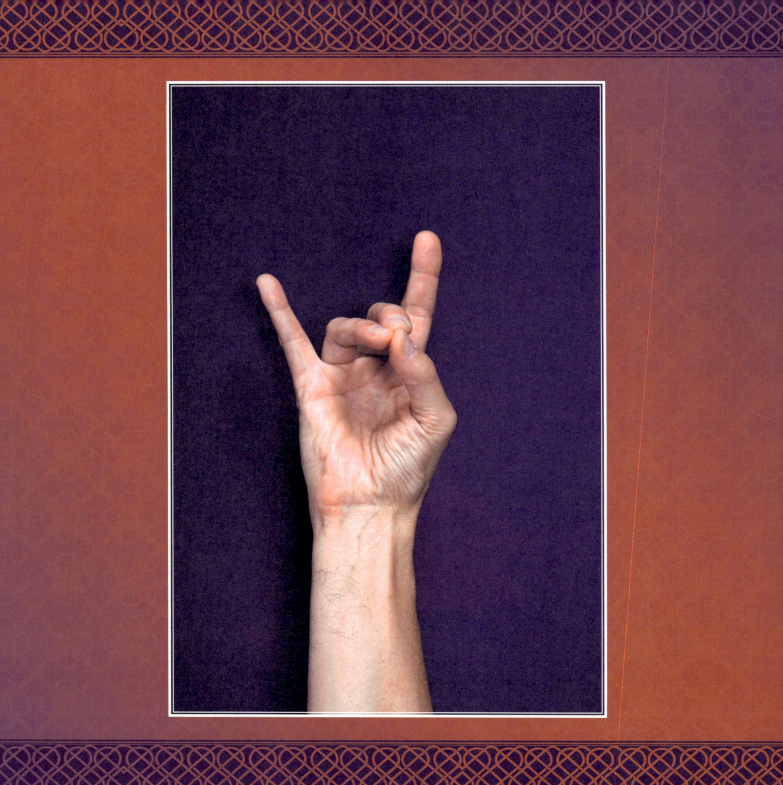

APANA

The tips of the ring and middle fingers gently touch the tip of the thumb. The other fingers are straight and pointing upwards.

- strengthens the kidneys

- treats diabetes

- removes toxins from the body

- brings peace of mind

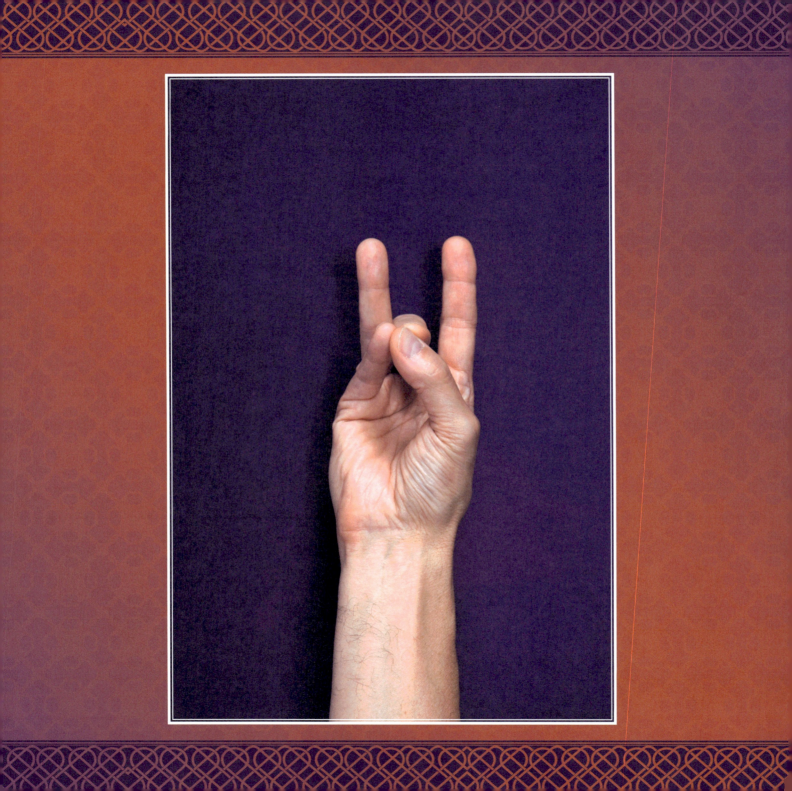

MERUDANDA

The tips of the little and middle fingers gently touch the tip of the thumb. The other fingers are straight and pointing upwards.

- treats back pain

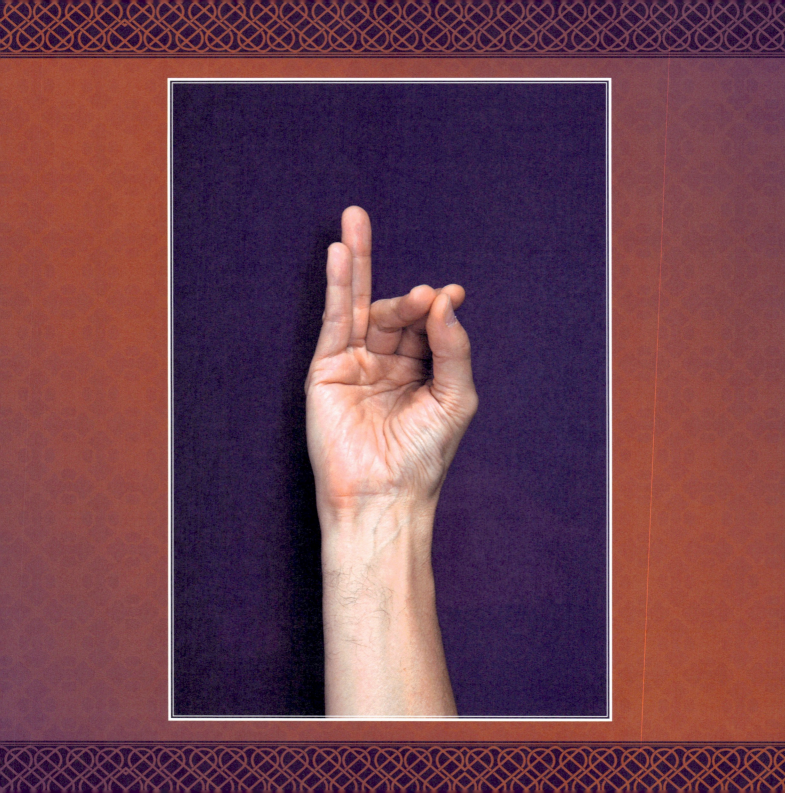

VYIANA

The tips of the index and middle fingers gently touch the tip of the thumb. The other fingers are straight and pointing upwards.

- helps concentration

- brings peace

- reduces mental tension

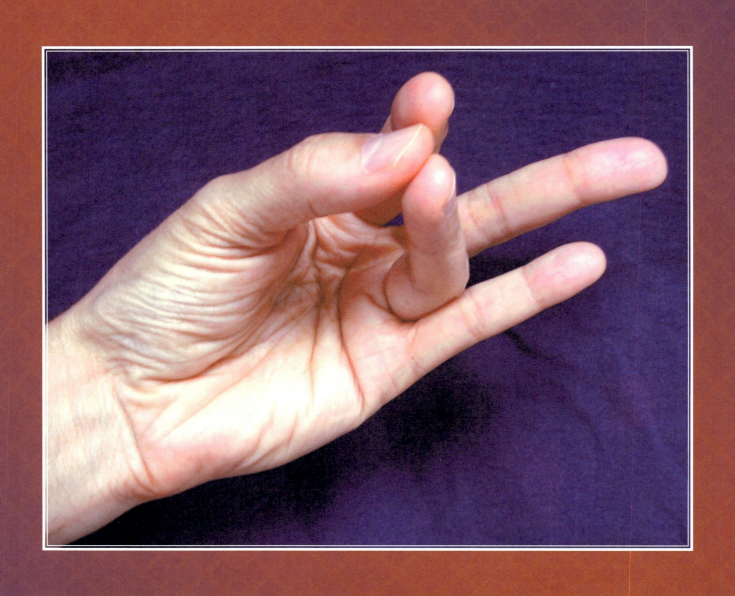

RUDRA

The tips of the index and ring fingers gently touch the tip of the thumb. The other fingers are straight.

- alleviates tiredness

- brings peace of mind

- strengthens the liver and the kidneys

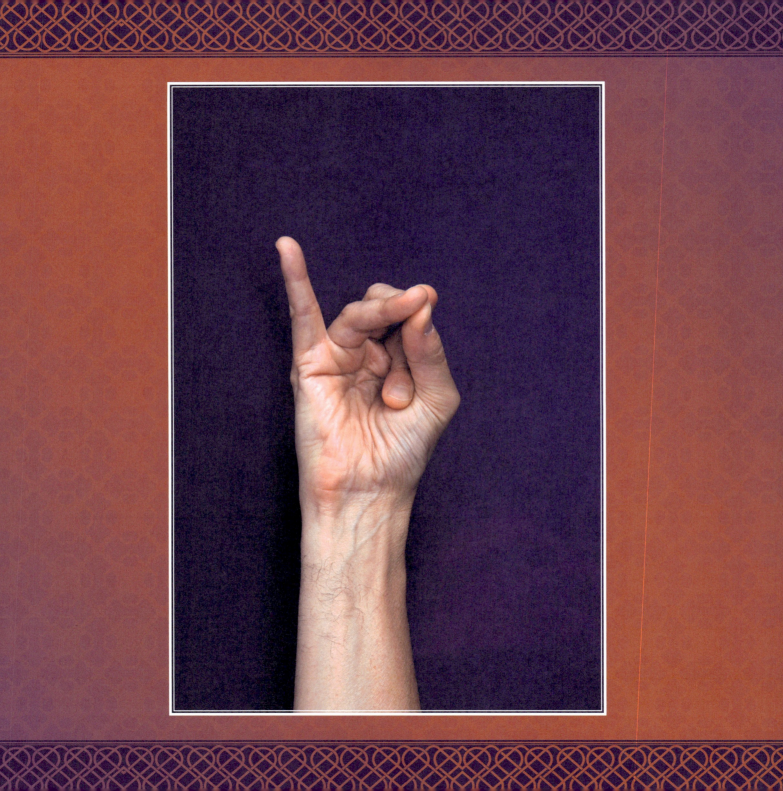

APANA VAYU

The index finger is bent, touching the base of the thumb, and the thumb is gently placed over it. The tips of the middle and ring fingers touch the tip of the thumb. The little finger is straight and pointing upwards.

- strengthens the heart

- useful in case of heart attack

- treats headaches, gastritis and constipation

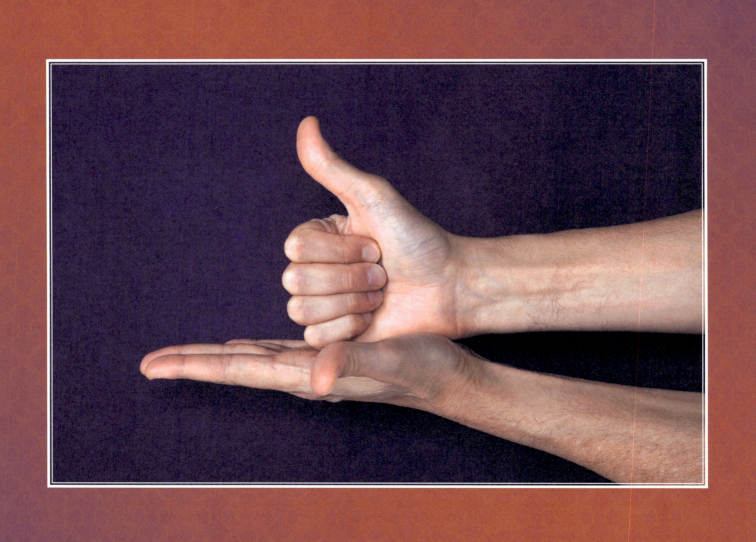

LINGA

The right hand makes a fist with the thumb outstretched and pointing upwards. The right hand rests on the palm of the left hand.

- generates heat in the body

- treats pneumonia, asthma, colds and cough

- promotes weight loss

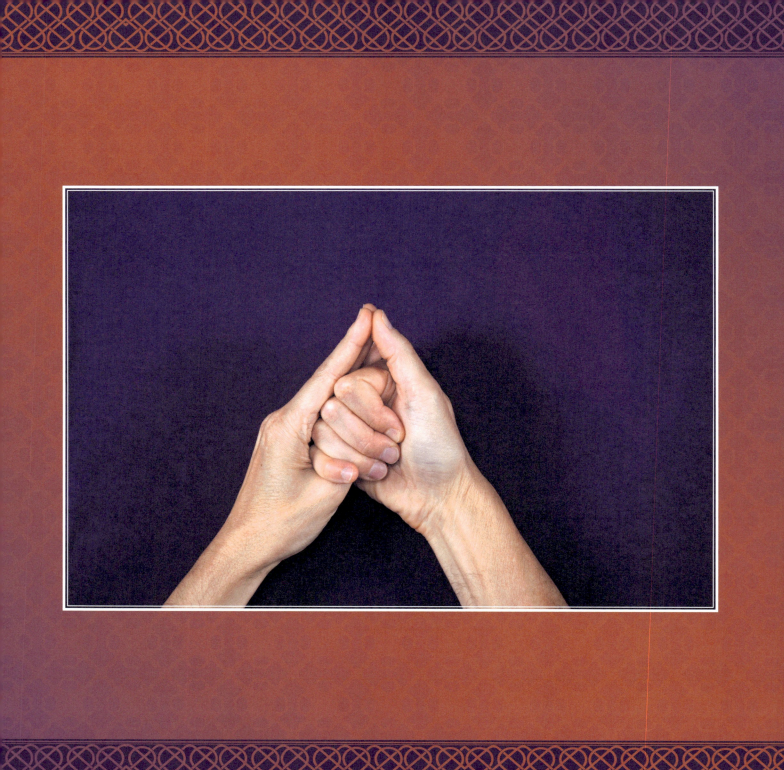

SHANKHA

The left thumb is placed in the center of the right palm and all four fingers of the right hand are wrapped around it. The tips of the fingers of the left hand touch the tip of the right thumb.

- treats gall bladder and intestinal disorders

- activates the thyroid gland

- improves the voice

- helps digestion

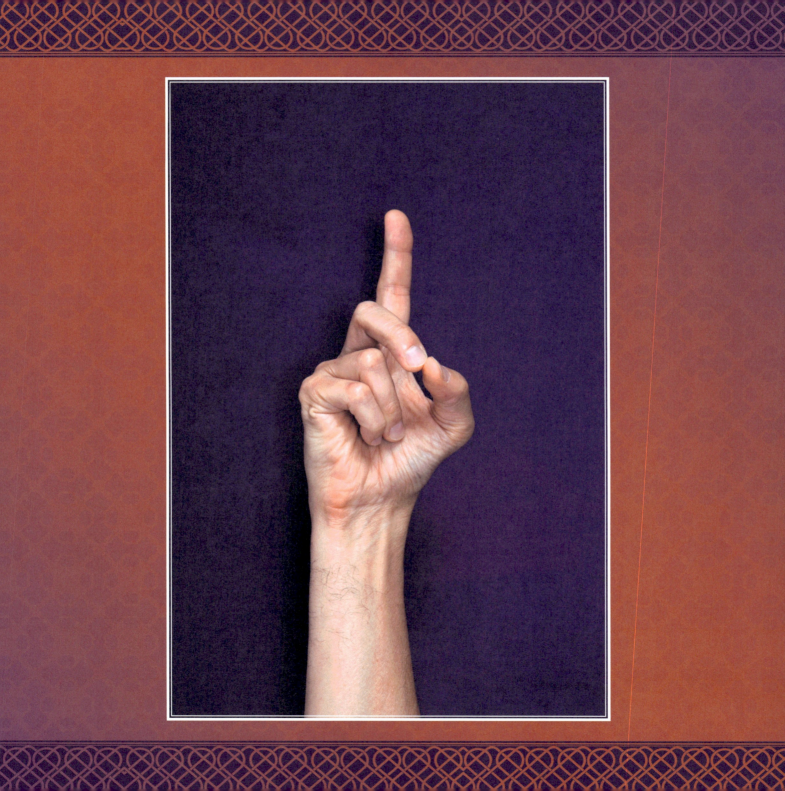

SHWAZA

The little and ring fingers are bent onto the palm of the hand while the tip of the middle finger gently touches the tip of the thumb. The index finger is straight and pointing upwards.

- treats asthma and other lung-related problems

- controls sadness

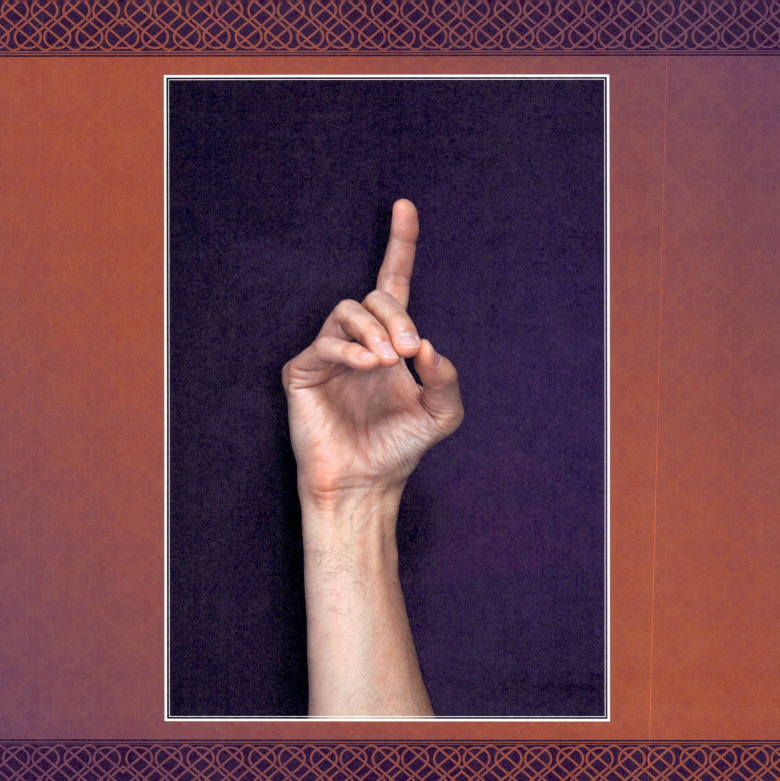

VRAJRA

The little, ring and middle fingers are brought together while the tip of the thumb gently touches the nail of the middle finger. The index finger is straight and pointing upwards.

- stimulates vitality

- controls high blood pressure

- strengthens the heart, stomach, spleen and pancreas

BRHAMARA

The index finger is bent, touching the base of the thumb, while the tip of the middle finger touches the tip of the thumb. The ring and little fingers are straight.

- increases body resistance

- treats allergies

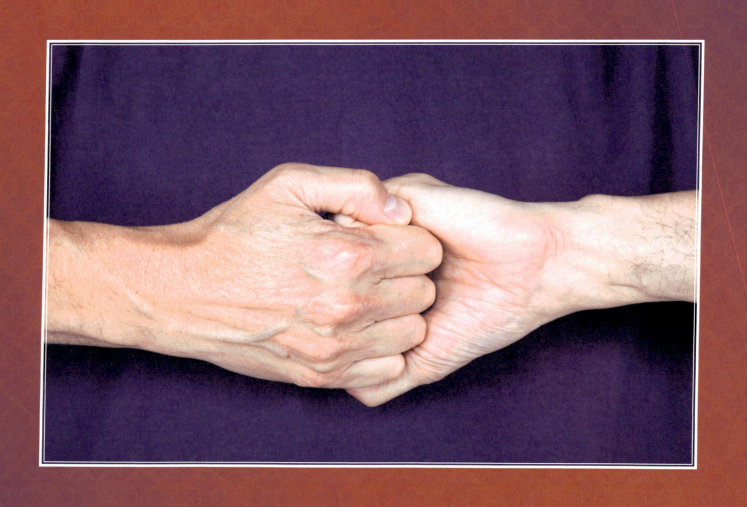

AGRAGAMI (GANESHA)

The fingers of both hands are interlocked. The hands are pulled in opposite directions upon exhalation.

- unblocks arteries and veins

- opens the bronchial tubes

- stimulates self-confidence and courage

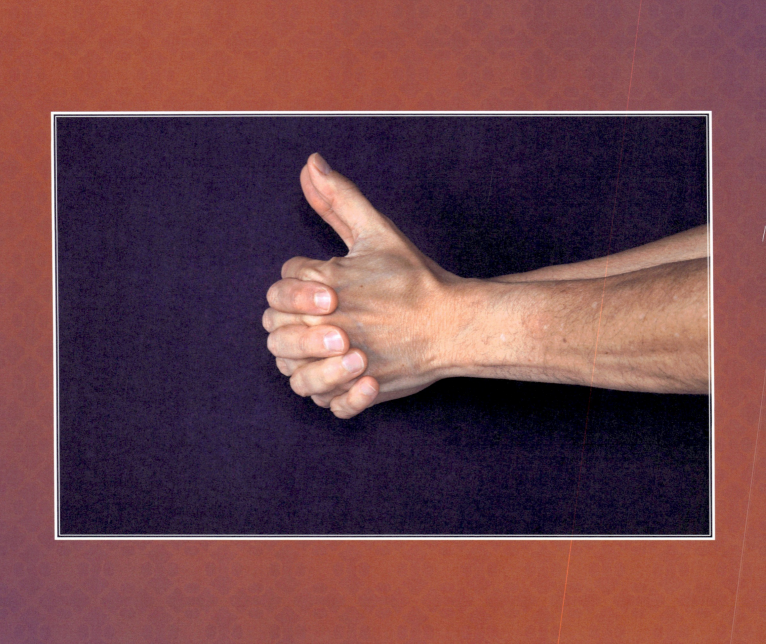

SAHAJA SHANKHA

The fingers of both hands are interlocked while the thumbs are kept together, pointing upwards.

- helps cure stammering

- improves a singer's voice

- treats indigestion and flatulence

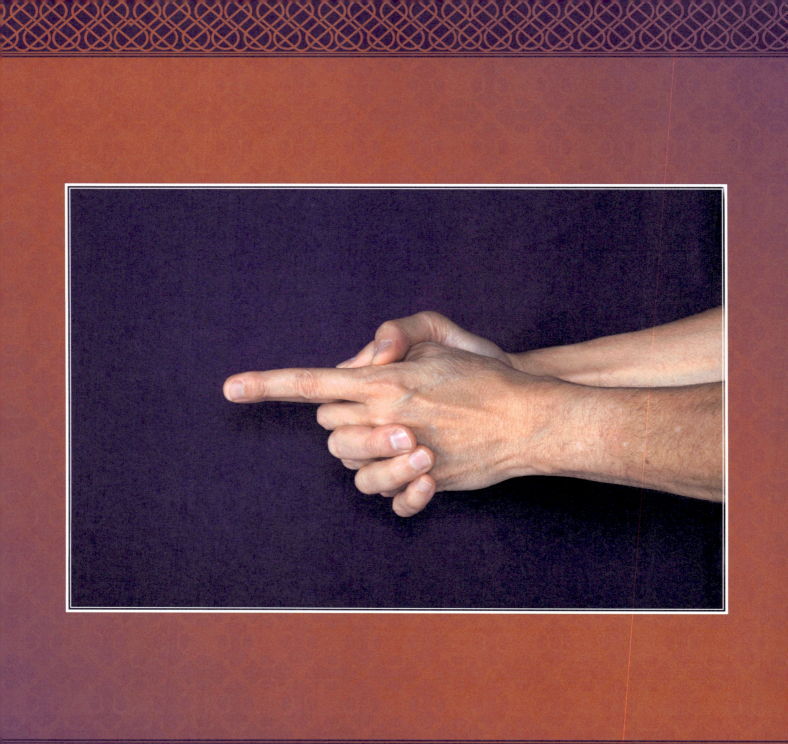

KSHEPANA

The fingers of both hands are interlocked while the two index fingers are kept together, pointing forward. The right thumb rests on top of the left thumb.

- strengthens the lungs and the large intestine

- promotes body cleansing

- improves the skin

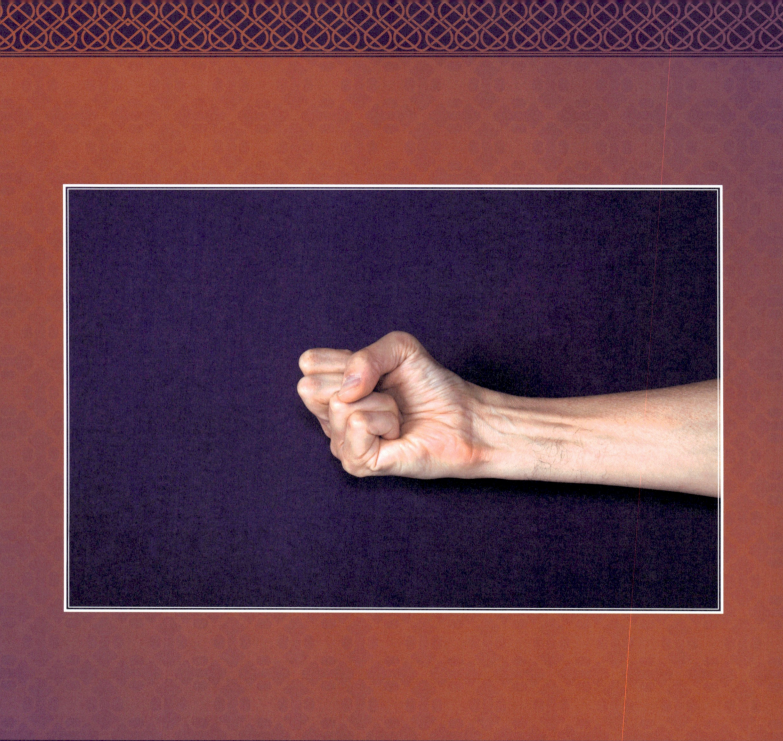

MUSHTI

A fist is made with the tip of the thumb resting gently on the ring finger.

- improves digestion

- treats constipation

HAKINI

The tips of the fingers of both hands are brought together. The three middle fingers point upwards while the thumbs and little fingers are held parallel to the ground.

- benefits the mind

- improves memory

- promotes balance between the brain's left and right hemispheres

- facilitates respiration

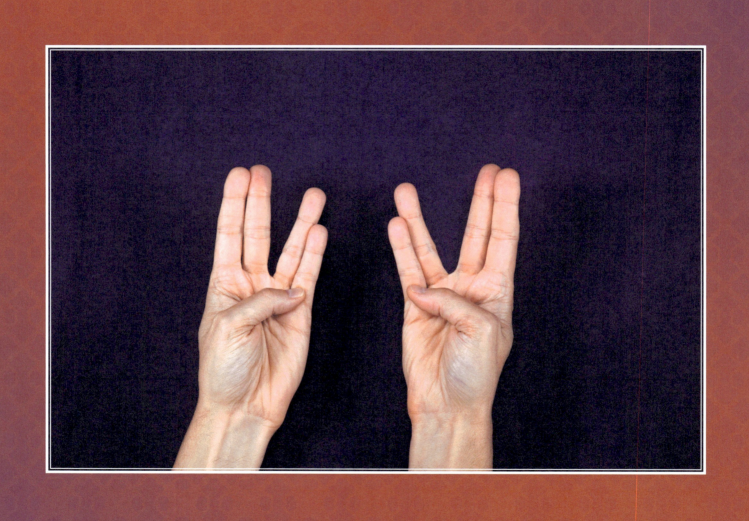

DETOX

The thumbs are bent to touch the space between the bases of the little and ring fingers. The other fingers are straight but relaxed.

- promotes detoxification of the body

SAKTI

The index and middle fingers of both hands are wrapped around the thumbs, while the tips of the ring and little fingers gently touch.

- has a calming effect

- promotes sleep

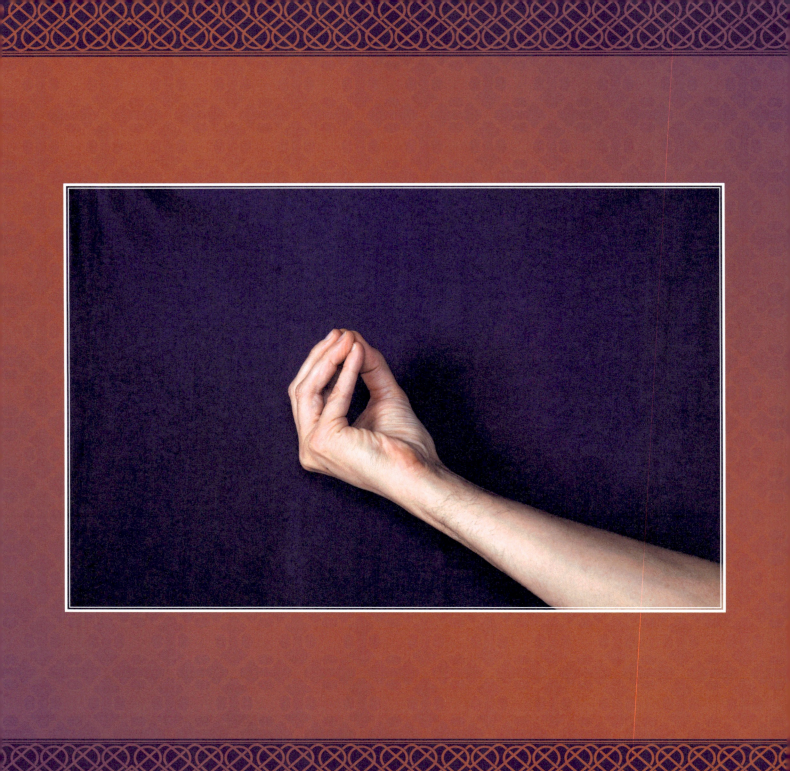

MUKULA

The tips of the four fingers gently touch the tip of the thumb.

- directs energy to parts of the body that are deficient

- brings relief when placed over tense or painful areas

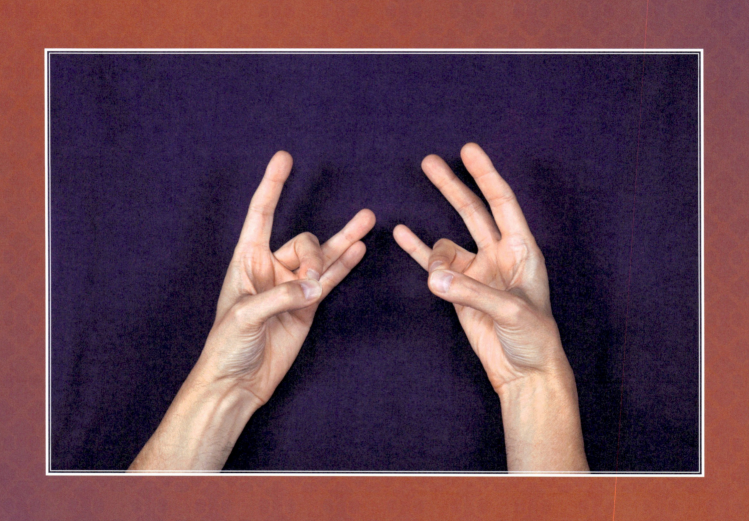

JOINT

On the right hand, the tip of the thumb gently touches the tip of the ring finger. On the left hand, the tip of the thumb gently touches the tip of the middle finger.

- improves the energy and movement of the joints

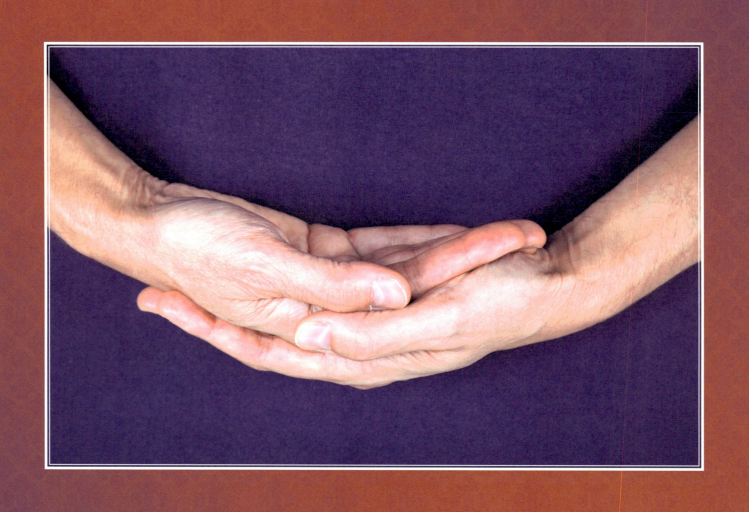

DHYNA

The right hand is gently placed over the left hand, with both hands facing upwards.

- benefits the thyroid gland and the heart

- improves general health

- balances blood pressure

- brings peace of mind

LOTUS

The tips of the thumbs and little fingers of each hand gently touch while the other fingers are separate and facing upwards.

- energizes the heart chakra

- alleviates despair and loneliness

- symbolizes purity

ANTHARATMA

The thumbs are brought together while the tips of the other fingers gently touch.

- helps to go deep within to reach the Divine

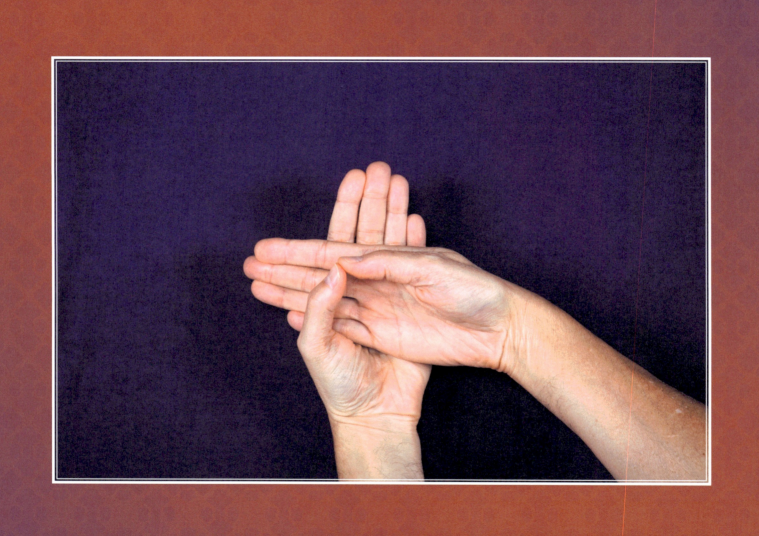

NAGA

The hands are crossed in front of the chest while the tips of the thumbs gently touch.

- helps to face everyday challenges

- assists in overcoming mental and spiritual obstacles

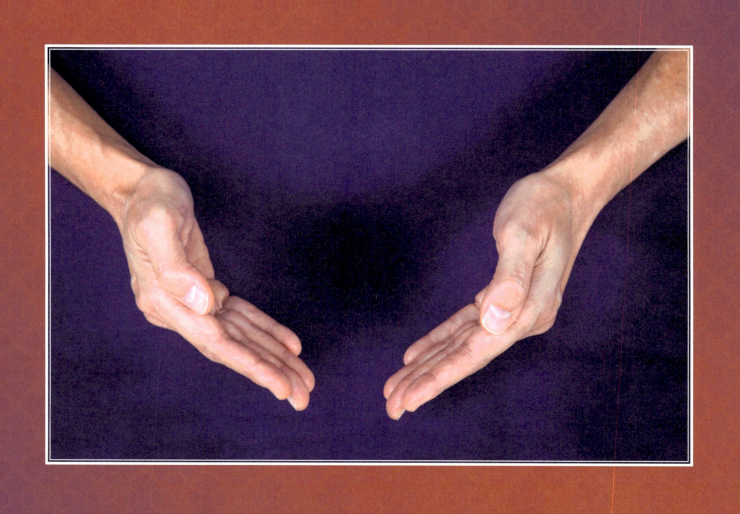

PUSHPA

The hands are cupped, facing each other and resting on the thighs.

- symbolizes opening and acceptance

- helps resolve negative emotions

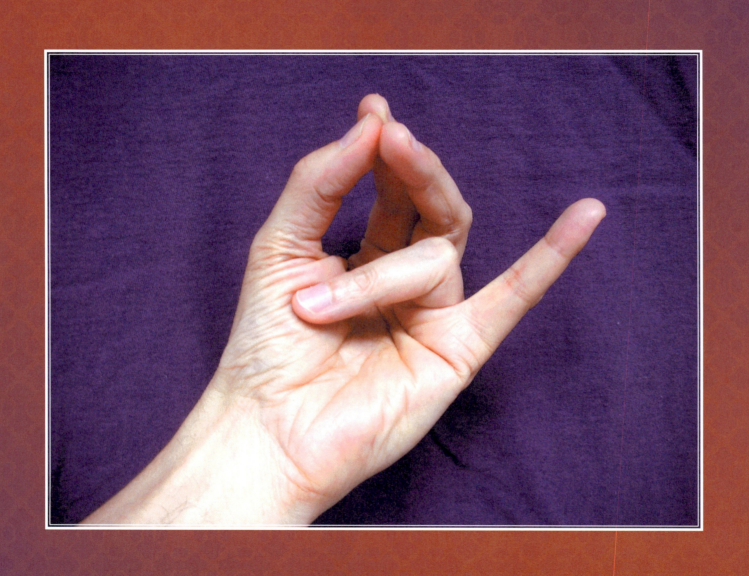

MAHASHEERSHA

**The tips of the index and middle fingers gently touch the tip of the thumb while the ring finger touches the base of the thumb.
The little finger is straight.**

- treats headaches, especially those caused by disturbance in the digestive system

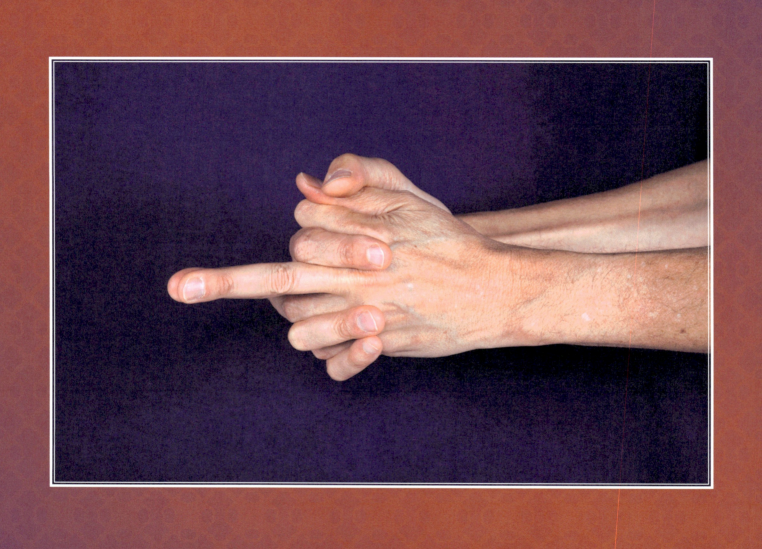

MATANGA

The hands are placed in front of the solar plexus. The fingers of both hands are interlocked while the two middle fingers are kept together, pointing forward. The right thumb rests on top of the left thumb.

- strengthens the heart, liver, gall bladder and kidneys

- tonifies the Earth Element

- pacifies the mind

- energizes the solar plexus and the respiratory system

DHYANI JNANAYOGA

The tips of the index fingers and thumbs of both hands gently touch. Facing upwards, the right hand is brought to rest on the left.

- brings peace of mind, purifies thoughts

- helps concentration

- harmonizes blood circulation (indicated for blood pressure and heart problems)

- strengthens the muscle system

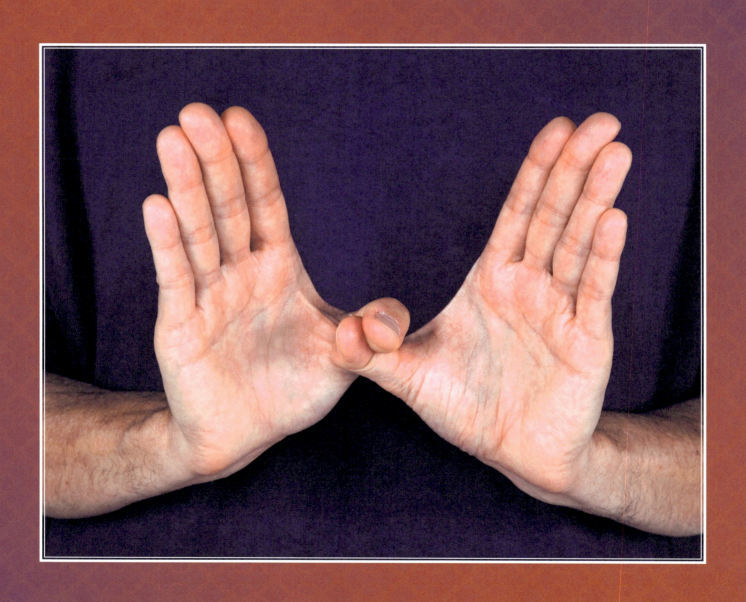

GARUDA

**The palms of the hands face outwards
with the thumbs interlocked.**

- treats irregular periods and digestive problems

- improves circulation

**Note: this mudra is not recommended for
those suffering from hypertension**

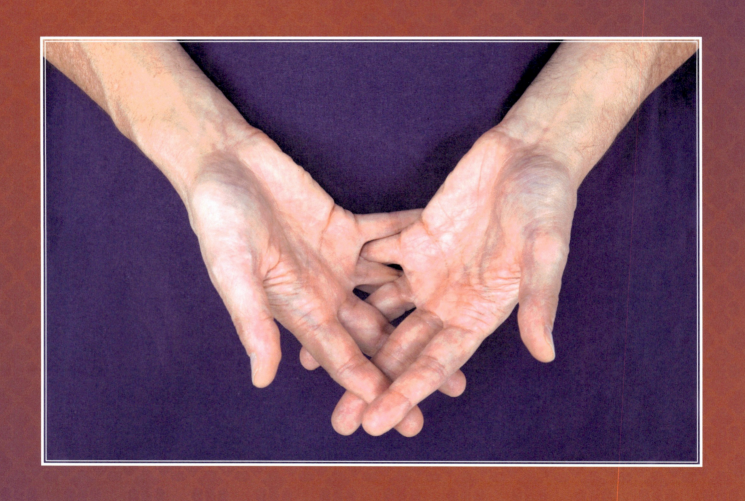

VAJRAPRADANA

The fingers of both hands are interlocked, with the palms facing upwards.

- improves self-confidence

- releases sadness and melancholy

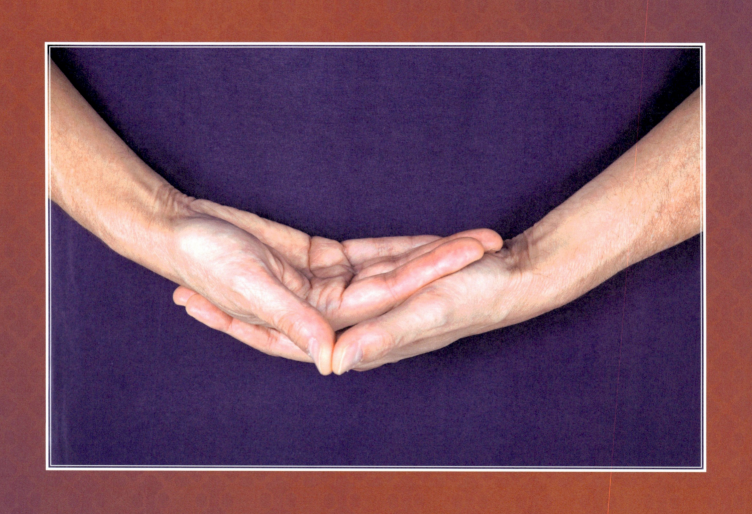

DHYANI

The right hand gently rests over the left hand. Both hands face upwards with the tips of the thumbs touching.

- meditation posture

- symbolizes openness to receive

- increases the energy flow in the hands

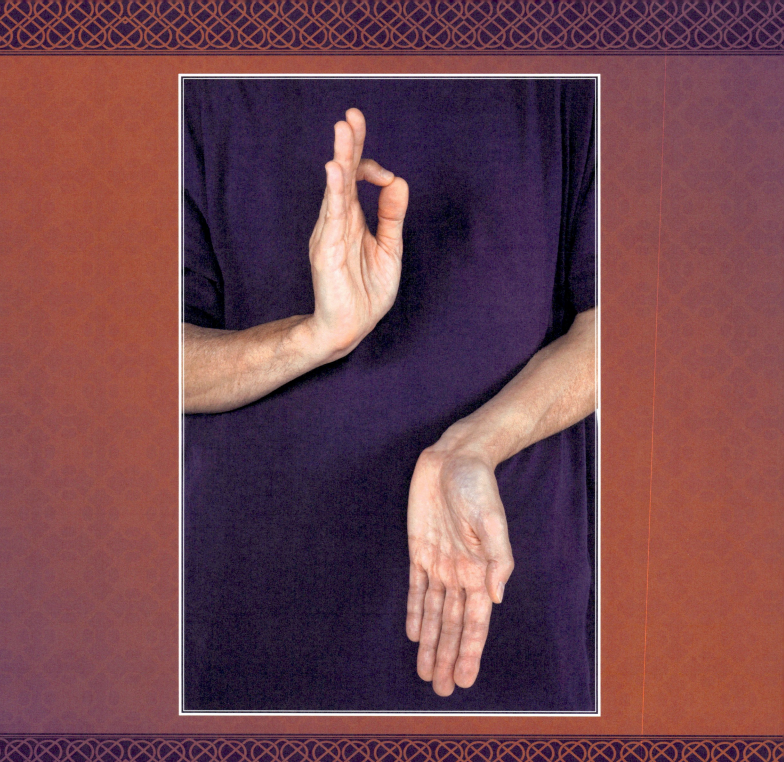

VIRTAKA

The right hand is held at the center of the chest, with the tip of the index finger gently touching the tip of the thumb and the other fingers pointing upwards. The left hand is placed below the right, facing outwards and pointing downwards.

- symbolizes teaching, sharing knowledge

Printed in the United States
By Bookmasters